You'll love again.

-Bernardo

KUN

Follow me @bernardocarbo
More stories coming
Find them on Amazon

KUN
THE HEARTBREAK
by Bernardo Carbó

Illustrated by
Derek López Vergara

The time I spent back home I did in my old room.
I was never really affectionate or tactful
towards my mom, so it came as a sweet surprise
when I asked her to cuddle and hug me.

It was a first.

"One sits oppressed under a bare tree and strays into a gloomy valley. For three years one sees nothing."

–I Ching

One morning I won't get out of bed.
People in my house will come to see
if I'm asleep, and by their sad eyes
I'll know I'm sick.

My mom will retell this as if it were a bedtime story:

A woman, recently divorced, insisted to her ex
that she would take the kids and move to Alaska.
The father fervently opposed. After dwelling on the subject
and arguing with no luck, she grabbed the children
and hopped on a plane which would later crash
in the Atlantic Ocean. While she was swimming
in the polar water and waiting for the rescue team,
she held on to her two sons.

"Mommy, mommy, I'm cold," cried one,
and he froze to death in her arms.
There was nothing else she could do,
so she let him sink to the bottom of the sea.
"Mommy, mommy, me too." An hour later
the other one followed the same fate,
and she watched him fall into the abyss.

Then, help arrived, and she was safe.

How did she forgive herself? I don't know.
They say one day she did.

I'll hear the wood floor creaking,
she'll have a bowl of warm oatmeal
in her hands.

"Don't open the curtains,
I want to sleep.
When I dream,
I'm happy again."

The evening fell and I had a knot in my stomach.
The offerings on my nightstand were stale and cold.
The smell of the juice was sour.
"You have to eat."
My body forced its will on my mind.

Sorrow with bread is easier to swallow.
I understood then.

Cats and dogs will sit solemnly by my side
as if I was terminally ill.

I'll start writing goodbye notes.

Wouldn't it be romantic to be remembered
for dying of love?

No. It would be cheesy and gross.

When our relationship ended,
my lungs broke into a screech
that caused people to come out
and see if I was hurt.

"Get over it!" a stranger yelled from afar
while my nose ran and bystanders gossiped.

Every night I lay in bed
with the same question I had during the day:
How can I fix this?

I never had anxiety
until I became fixated on fixing something
out of my reach.

It's like I had square pegs and round holes.
I swear there was a round peg.
I've seen one before!

My coworkers bought me a bouquet of roses
with a card signed by a secret admirer.
"You must be excited." They patted me on the back.
I didn't have an erection for a month,
not even when waking up.

When you are sick, your mind forgets
what it's like to be healthy.
When the fever is gone, you forget
what it's like to be sick.

I will scratch the couch
and my childhood habit
of biting my nails, will recur.

It's just like being an indoor cat.
Before knowing outside,
you're pretty content.
Once you've been on the other side,
you toss and turn while in the house.

I will let a teardrop splash
into someone's soup
right before I lock myself
in the breakroom.

"You're too pale to work,"
they will suggest
I take some time off.

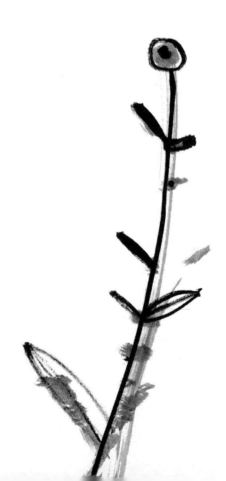

No one dies of HIV,
but another disease finishes the job.
No one dies of a broken heart,
but the suicide rates are high enough.

I will put on my gym clothes,
eat a protein bar,
and walk out to the porch,
where I will sit for an hour
staring at my phone.

The forty-year-old divorcée next door will witness it.

The construct of her in a non-flattering nightgown,
surrounded by horse throw pillows, sipping wine alone,
will drive me to beg you even more.

I set words like bridges:
"There will be rough times,
but we are there for each other."

And you tore them down:
"We are not married.
I owe you nothing."

The fear that grew inside
when you started resisting me.
If people can smell sadness,
I must have reeked despair.

I was envious
that you no longer wanted
or needed me.
I still wanted and needed you.

Envy is what we imagine.

I tried to hit back. I posted pictures
with forced smiles and pretend suitors.
Haha, I didn't have the privilege
of making you jealous.

At most, I only made it worse.

"You'll be given a restraining order
if you don't stop begging,"
friends cautioned me.

No matter how many round pegs
I had in my hands,
you only showed me square holes.

We were supposed to go to Italy,
stroll through streets full of history,
and give in to hedonistic pleasures.

Those empty plane seats with our names
became a torment. I don't want to go into detail.
It was hard enough to work at an Italian restaurant
and stare at that mural of Venice every day.

My friends gasped when they heard
I had spent all my savings on a trip
we never went on.

They said in ten years you will regret
leaving.

I don't have ten years.

You said "I love you" one day before you left me.
I knew I found that slippery tone of voice familiar.

When we were little,
my mom used to wake up early
and cook three bowls of oatmeal.
"Delicious." I deceived her with a smile.
She brushed her teeth
while I dumped the porridge in a plastic bag
and slung it out the window.

I will call you sometimes.
Your ego smirks at me
in a way
I feel foolish.

Why would I do that?
I'll scold myself five minutes later.

When a coyote falls into a trap,
it will gnaw its leg off to be free.

When we fall into an emotional trap,
our instinct is to sacrifice our dignity
even though we know the outcome.

I remember days
when scrubbing myself in the shower
would be the only touch,
and the sun on my skin, my only relief.

"Will you stay on the phone five more minutes?"
I asked every single friend.

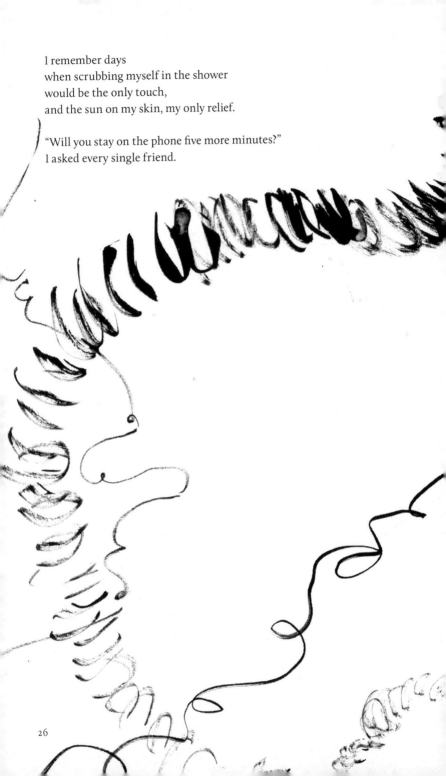

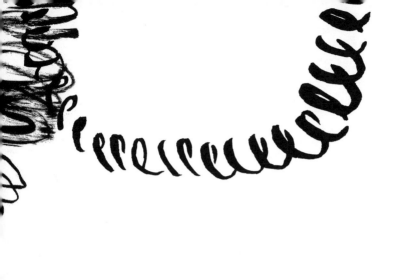

I held tight and kissed
that plush toy you gave me
until it was too denigrating
to cherish an unrequited love.

I slept with someone else. I cried in the bathroom afterwards.

Upon request, new acquaintances
took me climbing for the first time.

The wind was mischievous.
I gripped the rock
and the game of getting higher
became enough
to forget about the hurting.

Then, at the top,
all those pegs and what ifs flew back to attack me.

"What if I unclip myself and let go?
If it's an accident, it would be easier
on everyone."

I'll pay a visit to a psychiatrist.

"I want the pills"
will be the first sentence out of my mouth
willing to play in the cul-de-sac
of Western monsters.

The helping hand will open in wisdom:
"Harsh crises will come in unexpected shapes.
I rather you be anxious than doped."

"You should meditate."
They toss the term around
as if it were a pie ingredient.

Set your expectations low,
forgive and forget,
add gratitude as needed,
place yourself on a mat for 20 minutes,
and criss cross applesauce.
You're not depressed anymore.

I put on my running shoes,
leave my phone on the desk,
and go to the gym every morning.

I have my neighbor as my witness.
We wave enthusiastically while I jog
and she waters her garden.

To be mindful is like when you're chopping an onion.
Suddenly, this grey cloud overwhelms your brain
with squares and pegs and worries and losses.
Just look at the onion.
You're chopping an onion.
It's alright.

I chased down the cat to play.
He picked up the habit of hiding from me
whenever I walked through the door.

I shouldn't have asked for anything
that didn't come out of your will.
I didn't want it if the intention
was just to please me.

I did what I considered the best
with what was in front of me.

You did as well.

No blame.

I unpacked under an unknown ceiling,
and set up the presents you gave me
like a candid museum
for when you'd come back.

It was comforting to know
people were going through the exact same pain
five thousand years ago.

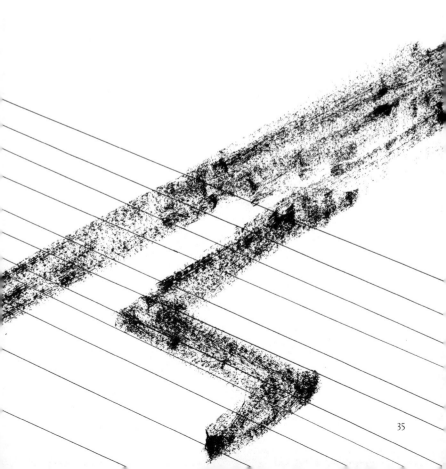

My brother laughed when I cried at our aunt's funeral,
not for her, for you.

He never lost it all.
His life,
his house,
his job,
his love,
his expectations,
all at once.

My brother said he would be able
to overcome the addiction if he ever tried heroin.

Please. He can't even handle himself
around a jar of peanut butter.

I asked my dad how he did it when he lost
his love,
his house,
his expectations.

"You're wondering whether or not I wanted
to jump off that building." He pointed at a fifth floor.

I nodded.

"You had school the next day,
and your brother had karate practice."

A motorcycle passed by and a flock of birds rose
from a power line where they had been accumulating.
With them, our attention.

I will visit the acupuncturist
in hopes of reducing the headache.
Exhausted and needled up
they will repeat an ancient proverb to me:

"In life you grab
and you let go."

It makes sense,
at least on paper.

I tried not to use my friends
as bottomless buckets
where I could throw up
my pain and anguish.
I excused myself at dinner parties
and hid away in remote alleys.

They say sad people stink
more than dead bodies.

I will lay my head down
and rest on the lap of a friend.
She will run her fingers through my hair
and the helping hand will open again:

"It is very disrespectful of you
to imply that your friends and family
are not enough to be happy."

Cats, like lovers, show up
when they want affection.

Dogs, like friends, know
a better kind of love.

Never put them in the same bag.

I wanted to be the same person
when the sky was falling.
Not for me, but for you.

How easy we twist and fight,
like a slug bathed in salt,
when we perceive change
as the enemy.

I went
knowing you didn't
want me
or need me
anymore.

I went to your work and you stood still,
waiting for me to leave.

I was conscious of my odds.
Don't bring me pity
like you would bring dinner scraps
wrapped in tinfoil to a homeless person.

I'll get nervous whenever I see
a parked car that looks like yours.

I'll rehearse a couple speeches,
but I won't come up with anything
that isn't compromising how I feel.

I will take the long way to work
to stop in front of the ice cream shop
where we had our first date.

"Stop torturing yourself,"
I will hear the voice of my mom in my head.

I will not have learned to let go,
but from then on,
I will cancel any plans that require me
to go out of my way
in a denigrating manner.

They told me once the happiest I've looked
was in a picture where you were kissing my cheek.

Nostalgia is a tricky game.
Your face is the one I loved,
but your heart and actions are different.

I don't trust you.

I stopped searching
'how to get your ex back'
and started typing
'how to stop loving someone'.

Why couldn't I let you go?
Were you that special
or did I just miss playing
with your dogs?

The list of things I liked about you
and the list of things I didn't
are only for me to know.

Not all drunk people tell the truth
but all drunk people make poor choices.

I'll call again.
My lack of inhibition
will most likely end up
in a complacent eye roll
from your side of the phone.

When I was younger,
I would peek through the curtains,
like a cat amused
by the squirming of a pray,
to see an ex begging.

I don't believe in karma,
but I do remember laughing
when I left someone else's heart broken.

In the middle of an empty highway,
I flipped my car and slashed my head.
My scalp flapped down like a dog's ear.
I walked drenched in blood,
convinced it was my last day.
A construction worker found me.

Later, strapped to a stretcher,
they told me it was a three hour drive
in an ambulance and that the gauze
didn't contain the hemorrhage.
I wasn't allowed to sleep,
so I requested music
to sing me away from this life.

I asked the EMT to call you, just you.
None of my friends needed my farewell.
They all knew I loved them.
Same for my dad and my brother.
My mom was in Poland, and I didn't want
to ruin her trip, so they were instructed
to contact her only if I passed.
I didn't want her to think I was indifferent
to her in my deathbed.

I'll see scabs washing down the drain
while softly patting the thirty two staples
in my half shaved head.
I won't be able to walk for a month,
the dizziness and swelling won't allow it.
I'll promise myself more days outdoors
when I recover.

You told me you wouldn't have called me
if you were about to die.
You told me I never cross your mind.

I forgave you.
I did it silently.
How stupid would I sound
for bringing up something
you didn't care about?

You really knew
how to twist the knife
to keep me far.
At least you were consistent.

I didn't know more about love than you did.
Neither did my songs, books, or friends.

Unconditional love is not a safe bet.
Ask mistreated moms.

I never thought you were a villain,
nor did I see myself as a victim.

I revisited our pictures,
kept like a shrine,
in a secret folder in my phone.

I went to bed with one question in mind:
What does this love mean to my life?

"He is oppressed
by creeping vines.
He moves uncertainly
and says, 'movement
brings remorse.'
If one feels remorse
over this and makes
a start, good
fortune comes."

–I Ching

The cat showed up before morning.
His paw on my forehead gently woke me up
to pet him.

I contemplated the gifts and reminiscences
of our relationship.

The day I fit everything that I could in a box,
I knew I was moving in the right direction.

I felt icky when the calendar revealed
how long I devoted to missing your presence.

It's not the time that heals,
it's the willingness to do so.
Emotions know no clock.

We all have become someone else's doormat
at some point.
The only thing that changes is for how long.

If you loved me or not is not important.

Unsolicited, I heard the sob story
of a friend whose ex wanted no more
than a few of her passwords.
I thought, how is it possible
to let someone treat you that way
and then defend them!

Twelve hours later I realized
I sounded just like her.
She won't listen either,
but I trust she'll recover.

They say the apology comes
when it's not wanted or needed.
As a species, we're forced
to rinse and repeat this cruel joke.

I'll catch myself skipping down the street
when no one is looking.

My upbeat self will come again
when I play songs that aren't about you.

My favorite part of pop music is that
it always delivers taoist brush strokes,
and in the most taoist fashion,
it never intends to do so.

They say I will love again.

I'm not in a rush but it's good to know.

In the early morning, good friends and I
went climbing. We did all summer.

They said I've never looked so happy.

I wouldn't compare my memories
to each other.
The reward we're promised
after letting go
is not something better,
just different.

At the top, pegs that had been accumulating
passed through my mind and soared into the clouds.

The sky falls and we become water.

Kun THE HEARTBREAK, first edition 2018
© 2018 Bernardo Carbó
ISBN: 978-1986543996

Written by Bernardo Carbó
Designed by Derek López Vergara
Thanks to Sarah, Mason, Tania,
and Arturo for their help.

Set in the typographic family Calluna
Printed with CreateSpace